10 Easy Breezy Ways to Boost Your Credit in 90 Days

Do It Yourself Guide for Free

By Yolanda Washington Cowan

10 Easy Breezy Ways to Boost Your Credit in 90 Days
Do It Yourself Guide for Free

All rights reserved
ISBN: 978-0-9601081-3-8
Published by
B-Inspired Publishing
7285 Winchester Road, Suite 109
Memphis, TN 38125
www.B-Inspiredpub.com
Printed in the United States
First Edition: September 2020

Table of Contents

INTRODUCTION 1

    WHAT IS A CREDIT SCORE?.. 3

    BENEFITS OF A GOOD SCORE: 4

CHAPTER 1: GET A COPY OF YOUR CREDIT CARD REPORTS WITH

YOUR FICO SCORES 6

    WHY IS IT IMPORTANT TO CHECK IT?... 6

    HOW YOU CAN GET THE REPORT: 7

    HOW TO READ A CREDIT REPORT? 8

    CREDIT REPORTS AND SCORES: 10

    FICO SCORE:.. 10

    THE RANGES OF A FICO SCORE: 11

CHAPTER 2: GET THOSE DEROGATORY REMARKS REMOVED 13

    THE MEANING OF DEROGATORY REMARKS: 14

    HOW DOES IT OCCUR:... 14

        Here are some more reasons that could lead to a

        derogatory remark on your credit report:......................... *15*

    HOW TO REMOVE THE DEROGATORY REMARKS? 17

        Collections-dispute:.. *17*

    HOW TO REMOVE A COLLECTION? 18

    LATE PAYMENTS OR MISPAYMENTS: 19

    STATUTE OF LIMITATIONS: 21

CHAPTER 3: NEGOTIATE COLLECTION PAST DUE BILLS 23

    HOW IS THAT POSSIBLE? 23

VERIFICATION: 24

   You have rights: 24

FIND THE KIND OF DEBT YOU OWE: 25

   For example: 25

   Take a look at hardship plans: 25

   A lump-sum offer: 26

   Mention Bankruptcy: 26

   The way you speak matters: 27

THE STATUTE OF LIMITATIONS: 27

NEGOTIATE THE REPORTING: 28

AGREEMENT IN WRITING: 28

CHAPTER 4: REDUCE CREDIT UTILIZATION 30

WHAT IS CREDIT UTILIZATION? 30

IMPORTANCE OF A REDUCED UTILIZATION: 30

HOW IT WORKS: 31

IS IT ALWAYS NECESSARY FOR IT TO BE LESS? 32

HOW TO REDUCE YOUR CREDIT UTILIZATION: 32

   Pay your credit bill: 32

   Ask for an increase of your credit limit: 33

   A new credit card: 34

   Refinancing with a personal loan: 35

CHAPTER 5: TAKE ADVANTAGE OF BALANCE TRANSFERS 36

THE WAY IT WORKS: 36

THE EFFECT OF BALANCE TRANSFERS ON A CREDIT SCORE: ... 37

MAKING ON-TIME PAYMENTS: 37

HARD INQUIRIES: 38

HOW THEY BALANCE OUT:..38

For example: 39

CHAPTER 6: BECOME AN **41**

AUTHORIZED USER **41**

WHAT IS AN AUTHORIZED USER?..41

THE EFFECT OF AN AUTHORIZED USER ON YOUR CREDIT SCORE:..........42

POSITIVE EFFECT:...43

NEGATIVE EFFECT:..43

THE EFFECT ON THE PRIMARY CARDHOLDER:................................44

HOW TO BECOME AN AUTHORIZED USER? 44

THINGS TO CONSIDER WHEN BECOMING AN AUTHORIZED USER:..........44

CHAPTER 7: GET SECURE CREDIT CARDS: **47**

WHAT IS A SECURED CARD?..47

HOW IT WORKS: 48

THE IMPACT OF IT ON YOUR CREDIT SCORE: 49

THINGS TO LOOK AT WHEN PURCHASING A SECURED CREDIT CARD:.....50

HOW TO USE IT EFFECTIVELY:...50

CHAPTER 8: USE FREE APPS TO HELP YOU MANAGE YOUR BOOST

YOUR SCORE **52**

MINT MONEY MANAGER: 52

DEBT TRACKER PRO:..53

CREDIT KARMA: 53

CREDIT.COM:...54

EXPERIAN:...55

TRANSUNION: 56

CHAPTER 9: HAVE HARD INQUIRIES REMOVED YOU DIDN'T ALLOW FOR PULLING YOUR CREDIT 57

THE IMPACT ON YOUR CREDIT SCORE: 58

REVIEW YOUR CREDIT REPORTS: 58

Now to check the incorrect hard inquiries, you need to focus on this section: 58

LOOK FOR THE UNAUTHORIZED OR INCORRECT HARD INQUIRY: 59

FILL IT WITH THE CORRESPONDING BUREAU: 61

CHAPTER 10: HAVE TAX LIENS THAT ARE PAID REMOVED 63

HOW TO REMOVE: 63

Appeal the lien: 63

The withdrawn of the linen: 64

Releasing the lien: 65

Lien subordination: 65

HOW TO AVOID: 66

YOU MUST HAVE PATIENT 67

Introduction

Boosting your credit score takes a lot of time, patience, and effort. However, by paying off debts and building new credit responsibly, you will be able to overcome financial mistakes to make use of excellent credit. Damaged credit rating and credit scores could throw a wrench into your life. You are going to have more difficulty obtaining loans and credit cards. If you receive a loan or credit card, you will often pay out a higher interest rate than individuals with credit ratings. You will not be qualified for charge cards with the best advantages and benefits. When you have lousy credit, do not despair, there are several approaches to start reversing your circumstances and put yourself on the path toward credit tender that is exceptional. There are significant steps required in repairing your credit: wait patiently, dispute credit report information, pay down debts, understand responsible credit habits and build new confidence, and assess your credit position. You need to identify why your credit scores dropped in the first place. You probably already have a good idea of what happened, whether you missed credit card payments or defaulted

on a personal loan. Regardless, taking a comprehensive, honest check out your financial situation is the initiative on the trail toward great credit. It also presents a valuable opportunity to identify and dispute incorrect information that could hurt your scores.

Chapter 1: Understanding Your FICO Score

A FICO score is a three-digit number used by financial institutions to determine your creditworthiness. The FICO score system was created by the Fair Isaac Corporation in 1989. It falls in the range between 300 to 850. Many lenders rate a credit score below 570 as bad credit. Then the lenders use this information to decide whether they should lend money to you or choose the risk of extending credit.

Your credit score is calculated by applying a mathematical algorithm to one of your three credit reports' information. These are updated regularly with the information that is available in your credit accounts. Now the real deal here is that your credit score is directly proportional to the readily available opportunities. This means that the higher your credit score is, the higher your chance is to get loans and that too, with the most favorable terms. This also includes:

-       Lower interest rates

-       Higher dollar amounts

-        A potentially lower fees

In general, developing an excellent credit score will open a lot of opportunities for you, and it will surely make your financial life a lot easier.

Benefits of a good score:

Here some of the great benefits that a good credit score will give you:

-        Lower interest rates: The interest is directly dependent on how good your credit score is, and it is the amount you pay for borrowing. A good credit score always enables you to get qualified for the best interest rates, and you pay off your debts in a much faster way.

-        Ease for rental houses and apartments: Nowadays, more landlords use credit scores as a part of their tenant screening. A bad credit score can damage your chances of getting into a new apartment.

-        Avoid security deposits: When you are relocating, you need to pay the security deposits on utilities. These can sometimes cost you 100-200 dollars. If you have a good credit score, then you don't have to worry about it.

-      Better car insurance rates: There is a high chance that auto insurers can use a bad credit score against you if you are thinking of buying a new car. With a good credit score, you generally pay less for insurance than similar applicants with lower credit scores.

To learn how you can increase your credit score, you need to read the following chapters. Without further ado, let's begin!

Chapter 1: Get A Copy Of Your Credit Card Reports With Your FICO Scores

The first and most vital step in increasing your credit score is to get a credit report. A credit report presents all the information your credit score holds. It is often advised to keep a regular check on your credit reports. A credit report is an ultimate resource that could positively impact your financial background. It helps reveal your personal payment history, lending, and creditworthiness.

Why is it important to check it?

Let's be honest. Nobody gives that much attention to their credit report. It is estimated that almost 32 % of individuals have never viewed a copy of their free credit report. You might not realize this sooner, but later it will lead you to more and more financial risks. Not reading your credit report is not the right way to take care of your financial health. You could cause yourself many problems which include:

- Can cost you money

- It can easily lead you to loans.

- It can also lead to credit denials.

- You have a higher chance of getting your identity stolen from fraudsters almost everywhere.

- It can also lead to a higher interest rate as you can miss the downtick.

- You can even lose job offers as some employers check your credit reports to get more information.

How you can get the report:

The best part about a credit report is that it is very readily available to almost everyone and is free. The three major credit bureaus will provide information about the company that may be considering a credit account.

You can get one free copy of your credit report every year from the three major credit bureaus:

- Equifax

- Experian

- Transunion

You need to ask them to give you these free copies, and the bureaus get through specific resources. Here I

have summarized the best resources from where you can get your free credit reports:

-    Annualcrditreport.com

-    Freecreditscore.com

-    Credit Karma

-    Credit Sesame

A credit report has all the records of your repayment history, debt, and credit management. It also contains all the necessary information about accounts, even if they have gone bankrupt and collections.

Another important thing regarding a credit report is that you must also know how to read them. You also need to understand it to make sure you're more financially stable and can boost your credit scores! As this is a complete guide, here is how you can read your credit report:

How to read a credit report?
Here is how you can read your credit report:

-    The first section is the identification section. This section contains all the personal information about yourself, which is used for your identification.

Remember that whatever information is mentioned in this section should strictly refer to you. Confirm all the relevant information that is mentioned in the report with your real-life experiences.

- The next section will be the credit history section. In this, you need to ensure that everything listed there is accurate.

- The next section is public records, and it is hard to find an error in this section, but you can scan it if you are in any doubt.

- The most important section for you in the context of your credit score is, in fact, the third section of your report. This is called the inquiry section. The thing that you need to notice is hard inquiries. When you apply for a credit card loan or a mortgage, hard inquiries are made.

- Hard inquiries can lead your credit score to drop a few points, and to avoid that, you need to make sure that you have given consent for a hard inquiry to your credit.

Credit reports and scores:

Even though you get a free copy of your credit report every 12 months, you do not get a copy of your credit score. A credit score is, in fact, just a formula that converts the information in your credit report into a three-digit formula. MyFICO.com is a free web series that lets you see your credit score. This is the most common form of credit score that is readily available.

FICO Score:

Fair Isaac Corporation is a software company that forms your credit scores. It is the most widely used method to see your credit scores. It is estimated that almost 90 % of top lenders use FICO scores to help them make credit decisions. FICO scores consider the following things when they are making your credit scores. The five main things are:

- Payment history

- The current level of indebtedness

- Types of credit used

- Length of the credit history

- New credit accounts

The ranges of a FICO score:

The factor determining whether you have a good score is the range in which it lies. Here is how you can know whether your score is good or bad:

Range (300-850)	Excellent	Good	Bad Score
740-850	☐		
670-739		☐	
300-579			☐

The above illustration is a general estimation of average scores. A score below the good range can cause problems when it comes to asking for loans, and the higher the score, the better it will be for you to attain opportunities.

To achieve a high FICO score, you must have a mix of credit accounts and excellent maintenance of payment history. If you had a hard time maintaining both, you shouldn't be surprised if your FICO score is very low. Your FICO score will not increase and become high overnight; you need to take gradual steps to do that.

Your FICO score is unique. Now your goal here is not to judge your credit score but to find ways to improve

them. You need to get a copy of your FICO score, and then you are ready to take the next step.

Chapter 2: Get Those Derogatory Remarks Removed

You now know how to read a credit report. This next step is correlated with the previous step. It would help if you kept in mind that your credit score is entirely based on the information on your credit report. If the information on your credit report is not accurate, then there is a high chance that your score may not be correct, either.

This could also portray your score as lower than it is. This is why it is crucial to get those derogatory remarks removed from your score. Your goal here is to improve your score to a higher point rather than a lower one; negative remarks could hurt your credit scores. This is why it is vital to get them removed.

As mentioned before, life is unpredictable, and you need to be prepared to encounter setbacks, but it is also essential to secure the future as much as possible. Indeed, the best way is to have a good credit score; for that reason, you need to fight the obstacles that will come your way, one of them being derogatory remarks.

The meaning of derogatory remarks:

Derogatory remarks are a hindrance to your good score. They are negative remarks indicating that you did not pay your loan on time or as agreed. They can be long-lasting as well. You can say that these derogatory comments will stay on your credit report for up to 7 years, at least. An example of a derogatory remark would be bankruptcy. The biggest drawback that derogatory ratings give you is that they can also cause you a lot of damage because they can last so many years on your credit report. It can even go up to 10 years and beyond it.

A lower score with a derogatory remark is the worst scenario you could have in your financial situation.

How does it occur:

The question is how can a derogatory mark occur on your report card? There are two possible ways through which there is a possibility that you will have a derogatory remark on your report.

-        Negative information through a creditor given to the credit bureaus could be a reason for a derogatory remark regarding whatever negative report the creditor will provide; it will appear as an

unfavorable mark on your credit record after its translation.

-       If there is a public record added to your report by the credit bureaus, then there is a chance that it will appear as a derogated remark.

Considering the prevailing situation, you don't have to worry much about the public records section recently; there has been a public statement that the credit bureaus will see fewer tax liens and civil judgments on the credit reports.

Here are some more reasons that could lead to a derogatory remark on your credit report:

-       Late payments: an account payment way past the due date

-       Charge off: this happens after several missed payments, and the creditor thinks you will not pay further payments.

-       Bankruptcy: it's a legal proceeding

-       Civil judgment: this occurs when you lose a civil lawsuit

- Debt settlement: this happens when you only agree to pay half of your debt even after making a deal with the creditor

- Foreclosure: this happens when you miss many of your mortgages

- Tax lien: this happens when you fail to pay your tax.

Every reason mentioned above could stay up to 7 years or more on your credit report as a derogatory remark. When you remove this negative information, your score will increase. In some cases, these remarks are not even your fault; in fact, the credit bureaus are the ones who need to be blamed for misreporting false information.

In the past, people had to write letters to the credit bureaus to submit their queries. Computer technology has made it significantly more manageable and convenient for consumers to do it online.

How to remove the derogatory remarks?

Here is how you can remove your derogatory remarks by following the steps mentioned below.

Collections-dispute:

It is your right to have an accurate credit report. Due to this, you can easily discuss the errors with the credit bureau. You have the right to dispute almost anything that you find inaccurate, but the credit bureau will investigate first, and then they will delete the things that only the law allows them to delete.

Here is a list of the following items that you can dispute:

- Inaccurate items

- Incomplete items

- Outdated items

- Unverified items

- Misinformation about late payments

- Accounts that aren't yours

- A credit limit or an inaccurate loan

- An inaccurate creditor

- If the status of the account is inaccurate

How to remove a collection?

If a collection account is inaccurate or outdated, you can quickly get it removed by following these steps:

- First, you need to check all your credit reports. This will make you figure out the real cause of this misleading information. You will see where this information was reported from.

- You then must check the account's legitimacy, as some accounts might not get removed. The requirement should be that the account should be incorrect, and it should have been cleared a long time ago.

- After gaining knowledge of those things, it is time to decide what strategy you will adopt to file the dispute.

- In case of an inaccurate account, you need to dispute it with the credit bureau reporting it. You can file it online; Credit Karma is a great site.

- If a legitimate account has been paid for, you need to contact the collection agency to request a goodwill adjustment. I would recommend the last option first, as this one might not work the way the first one will, but it is better to give it a shot.

- It will take time and patience as these collections are being removed. It is not going to happen overnight.

Late payments or Mispayments:

Late payments can also cause problems with your credit score, and as you know by now, they can stay for up to 7 years on your credit report. The good thing is that you can dispute them.

Here I have summarized the three most effective ways to easily remove late payments from your credit report.

- You need to request a goodwill adjustment from the creditor, and most of the time, the creditors willingly and very happily grant you a goodwill adjustment. It will be more effective if your previous credit score is well-kept and in good condition.

- You can also call and ask them to remove the late payments sophisticatedly, but I would recommend the goodwill adjustment more.

- I have also heard about another method in which the creditors remove the late payment if you sign up for automatic payments in exchange.

Inaccurate information:

If there are errors and inaccurate information on your credit report, you can easily get it removed by following these steps.

- First, you need to obtain all your credit reports.

- Secondly, observe the inaccuracies that can be removed, but as mentioned before, the credit bureau only lets you remove the ones that are accurate in law; consider the following inaccuracies the most, wrong information, duplicate information, and negative information.

- The next step is to dispute, which you can do online or even write a letter to the credit bureau and call them. Just make sure that you mention the error accurately and give your identification.

-       The next step is to wait for at least 30 days.

Statute of limitations:

You charged off debts. This is another major and common derogatory remark on your credit report. Charged-off debts are a relatively more rigid form of a comment to dispute from your credit history. Still, as long you can consider a few things, The statute of limitations is the amount of time in which a creditor or a debt collector can make you pay the debt by using the court's force.

-       You need to look at your statute of limitations and determine the activity's last day.

-       Then, you need to contact the original creditor.

-       You can either call them or mail them, but you need to be sure that whatever information you provide them should be accurate as it can also be used against you.

These were the most common derogatory remarks that people encountered themselves with. Just follow the steps mentioned above, and you will surely be able to dispute the misleading information. To get a detailed look at debts and become debt-free, you can

gain knowledge through another book called '10 Ways to be debt free.

It is time for you to take the next step toward an increased credit score.

Chapter 3: Negotiate Collection Past Due Bills

If you have ever been called by a debt collector and felt overly stressed, you are not alone, as debt collectors can be extremely stressful for a couple of reasons. Suppose you already have debts in the past. In that case, the debt collectors could make the situation even worse as they can turn out to be overbearing and even abusive sometimes when they are talking about your financial history.

The thing is that because debt collectors and collection agencies can be stressful, people usually avoid getting involved with such people. They would prefer to go through any stressful time except to talk with the collection agencies.

Now, as ironic as it sounds, you can negotiate with collecting agencies and makeup an agreement to pay less than what you owe.

How is that possible?
The reason for this is obvious; however, the original debt that the agency bought from your creditor was in the form of some substantial discount. Now they don't

need to recover the entire amount to make a profit. You can propose a settlement, which is a win-win situation for you and the collector. You can pay off the debt quickly and lower the original amount.

Negotiating is the ideal way to deal with debt collectors as it does the job and provides you with benefits such as paying a lesser amount and too quickly.

Here are the steps you need to follow when negotiating with a collector.

Verification:

Firstly, if you get a call from a debt collector or a collecting agency informing you about the unpaid debt, you need to ensure that the debt is indeed yours and is a verified collecting agency. You can even ask them to send you a verification letter; if you don't receive it, know something isn't right.

You have rights:

You have rights when it comes to debts, and as a civilized citizen, you need to be aware of your rights to avoid any misbehavior by the collectors. These are your laws:

- The collector cannot lie to you.

- The collector cannot threaten to arrest or deport you from the state.

- The collector cannot call you before 8 am or after 9 pm.

- The collector cannot harass you.

- The collector cannot use profane language.

Find the kind of debt you owe:

You need to figure out the type of debt you owe. There could be various options, such as student loan debt, medical debt, credit card debt, etc. Finding the kind of debt, you owe will help you solve the problem more efficiently.

For example:

If you owe student loans, there is a chance that you will be able to work with your student loan service provider. In this way, you can get an income-based payment plan.

Look at hardship plans:

Now that you are aware that the debts are yours and the debt collector is not a fraud and is legitimate, then

the next thing you need to look forward to is to look at the hardship plans. This is a great technique, mainly if you rely on government assistance. Once the collector knows that your only source of income is through the government, they will stop contacting you.

A lump-sum offer:

No debt collectors are not always very unfriendly. There is a chance that a collector might agree to negotiate with you to score at least a partial repayment instead of nothing at all. As a debtor, it is your choice whether to tell them you want to give a lump sum or another repayment plan. This is a better option. As an estimated amount, the collector may settle for 50 % of the bill. You need to make sure you can make the new repayment arrangements you have agreed to.

Mention Bankruptcy:

Mentioning bankruptcy is another great strategy that could be used to negotiate with the collector. This will work for you if you have unsecured debt. Unsecured debt is not related to any assets, including your house or car. In this case, you can mention that you are filing for bankruptcy. This can reduce the debt liability, and

the collector will know that. The key here is not to portray foiling the bankruptcy as a threat.

The way you speak matters:

Your body language and how you speak to the collector also matter. Remember that you are trying to negotiate, and for that reason, you need to be calm, and when you're speaking statements that support your case, you need to make sure that those statements are relevant to your circumstances. The remarks should be logical. This is important because, as you know, debt collectors are known to create feelings of fear and worry inside you. You don't want that, as your strategy here is negotiating with the collector.

You should be very aware of your rights as a debtor, and the collector has a debt collector. Keep those things in mind and try to converse calmly and confidently. Find out the strategy that you will adopt for repayment.

The statute of limitations:

You should be aware of the statute of limitations. They can turn out to complicate your situation. This is why you must be knowledgeable of the statute of

limitations. Because the debt that your collector is trying to collect from has surpassed its actual day of payment, then there is a chance that the collector can sue you for that. Now when this happens, the whole process must start new. If you ended up paying for the debt past the statute of limitations, you would have to pay again. It is even better to consult an attorney if you encounter yourself in such a position.

Negotiate the reporting:

Your goal is to dispute all the negative information about your credit report's financial habits. If you agree to settle the debt, you need to politely ask the creditor how they will report this to the credit bureaus. You then have to request them to remove the negative information. The most reliable source would be if you get it written on a piece of paper by them.

Agreement in writing:

In case the negotiation is carried out for any new repayment or any additional changes, you need to get the settlement agreement in writing, and after that, it should be delivered to you. Get it mailed to your house.

This negotiation strategy will work for you. The next step is to reduce your credit utilization.

Chapter 4: Reduce Credit Utilization

Another key factor determining your credit score is the credit utilization ratio. Indeed, it would help if you improved credit utilization by reducing it. Still, before that, you need to understand the credit utilization ratio and how it operates and works.

What is credit utilization?

Credit utilization is the ratio of outstanding credit card balances to your credit card limits. What this does is it measures the available amount of credit that you are using. If you have ever encountered yourself in a position in which, after using your credit card, you see that there is no balance in it, then this means that your credit utilization would be zero. Now, if there is more than one card you are carrying around and using the balance, you are utilizing some of your credit. When this happens, the creditors take notes instantly.

Importance of a reduced utilization:

As you know, FICO is the leading agency you take help from when you want to determine your credit score, and they have said that credit utilization is the second

highest factor they see when determining your credit score.

In this case, if your credit utilization is high, it will lead to the idea that you are overspending, which is not a good impression, especially if you are looking forward to a higher credit score.

How it works:

To calculate your credit utilization ratio, you divide your credit card balance by your credit limit and multiply it by 100.

Credit utilization rate: your total debt/your full available credit

The ideal credit utilization = In a FICO score, keeping your credit utilization score below 30 % is commonly recommended. This is a general rule of thumb to stay below 30 %. This is advised for every card and the total amount of your credit utilization ratio. The thing here is that if the percentage is above 30 %, then it can decrease your credit score.

This will also give the lenders the impression that you are overspending way too much, and you will have a

hard time repaying the new debt to them. Credit utilization ratios also vary from age to age.

I recommend keeping your credit utilization ratio from 5 %-20%.

Is it always necessary for it to be less?

Keeping the utilization low doesn't mean you completely start ignoring your credit cards. Generally, credit scoring companies prefer 1 % to 0 %. It is advised to pay after the statement has been generated. If you pay before that, your next balance statement will show 0 %, indicating that your accounts are inactive after they are reported to the credit bureaus. It is better if you pay your entire statement balance. The ultimate way to do it is by making a partial payment.

How to reduce your credit utilization:

Here are the steps to improve your credit utilization by keeping them at an ideal reduced rate.

Pay your credit bill:

There is a closing date for the statement of your balance. The creditors report your credit card balances to the credit bureaus after the closing date. This means that they send the report based on the

statement balance. Now what the credit bureaus do is they use this information to calculate your credit utilization. This case may vary depending on the reporting dates, which can be different.

The key here is that you need to start paying smaller amounts more frequently instead of paying larger payments at once. This way, when you continue to pay in small installments, your credit utilization will be low.

Ask for an increase in your credit limit:

Asking for an increased credit card limit is also a great technique if you might not stay below the 30 percent ratio. There is an 89 percent chance that your request for an increased credit card limit will be accepted. This is a great way to reduce your credit utilization as well. This would create a big difference in your credit score as well.

Most card issuers accept the consumers' requests online, but you can also ask them on-call to increase your credit limit.

For example:

If you have a balance of $ 6,000 on a card with an $ 8000 limit, if the limit gets increased to $12,000, then this will reduce your credit utilization ratio.

A new credit card:

Now, this is another way to get a higher credit limit. All you need to do is to apply for another card. When you open another credit card, that card's credit limit will increase your credit limit, which will decrease your credit utilization.

This is more straightforward because you must apply for a card you qualify for. I recommend using a balance transfer card as you can even transfer your debt to that card.

It would help to be careful of this strategy, as more credit cards can lead to more spending temptations. This can lead you back from where you started and with even more increased credit utilization. So, you need to be very cautious of this step and adopt proper measures to avoid getting into such situations.

Refinancing with a personal loan:

Refinancing your debt with a personal loan is also a great way to consolidate credit card debt. It will give you a lower interest rate. You can also avail yourself of the opportunity of paying off your debt in a fixed amount each month. This will overall create a great impression on your credit score. You only need to get a loan for the full amount of credit card debt you have, and then you will use that loan to pay off your credit cards.

It can even bring it down to zero, but you need to be careful about not getting into overspending as it will cause only negative effects on your financial health. It works best if you pay off your debt after consolidating it.

This was how you could reduce your credit utilization to increase your score. The next step is how you can take advantage of balance transfers.

Chapter 5: Take Advantage of Balance Transfers

Balance transfers allow you to move your existing balances to new accounts. Now, this is an excellent opportunity to secure interest rates. Some credit card transfers can also offer you a zero percent utilization ratio of your credit. When you transfer an account with high-interest rates to an account with lower interest rates, you tend to reduce the borrowing's overall cost. This will help you clear your debt in a much faster way.

This is an effective money-saving method, especially with expensive credit debts. All your payment goes towards the monthly principal balance instead of the interest charges.

The way it works:

Your debt on your old card gets removed when you take out a balance credit card. The new balance clears out the old debt. This will allow a new account if yours have a lower interest.

Most balance transfer accounts also have the option of interest-free introductory offers on their credit cards.

If there is a promotional period, you will not be subjected to any interest. This could be as long as a period of 3 years.

Your credit card principal will get cleared because of all the repayments that will occur. The key here is to clear your balance within the interest-free limit. This way, you will repay your debts faster and with a zero-interest rate.

Now, if you do not manage to pay within the interest-free period, then it is obvious that you will have to pay with interest. Always make your payment on time in a bank transfer. This is why paying your debts within the promotional period is better. The key here is to pay more than the minimum amount.

The effect of balance transfers on a credit score:

It would help if you considered a few things and their impact on your overall credit score.

Making On-Time Payments:

If you have opted for a bank transfer credit card, you are familiar with a credit card's general use. The most important thing for credit card users is to make their payments on time. You need to operate the bank

transfers credit in the same way you know that your payment history does count in your credit score. It is estimated that your payment history is kept at almost 35 % in consideration when evaluating your credit score.

With a balance transfer card, it is easy to pay on time as you cannot apply for interest for at least the next three years. If you miss a payment, you will miss out on the 0 % interest rate, which is the introductory promotion.

Hard Inquiries:

Applying for a new credit card will portray a hard inquiry on your credit report, even if it's a bank transfer card. Now, as you know that hard inquiries are the ones that give a negative impression on your credit reports to the credit bureaus; they may lower your credit score by a few points.

How they balance out:

Despite this one adverse effect, it can balance the situation with an appositive effect. As mentioned before, opening a new credit card automatically increases your credit card limit. When you have an increased credit limit, your credit utilization gets

reduced. This is great as a reduced credit utilization ratio is favorable for a good score. The key here is that when your old balance returns to zero, it is important not to pile it up with debt. This will have a positive impact on your score.

For example:

If you are a student saddled with debt, you can consider getting a bank transfer credit as it has the option to lend you a student loan. The only thing that you need to keep in mind is to be realistic about your habits and situations. Make sure that you will be able to make the payments till the time there is zero interest.

Most credit cards charge almost 3 %- 5% of the balance you intend to transfer. So, if you want to lend a student loan of $ 5000, it will cost you $ 150. You can even adapt to the same technique if you are willing to purchase a new car. Remember that you cannot transfer all the credit limits into the new card.

Once your balance transfers are complete, the next thing is maintaining credit to stay healthy. Here are a few tips that can help you in avoiding any setbacks that could come your way:

-        You need to keep your accounts' average age high, so you shouldn't close your old accounts.

-        Apply for new credit when there is only an urgent need to do so, as you know that new credit could create hard inquiries on your credit reports. It's better if you apply if it's necessary.

-        Avoid making purchases with your balance transfer cards.

-        Make all your mothy payments on time, and you can even set your automatic payments from your account if you tend to forget easily.

-        Track your spending regularly and make a budget for yourself to not exceed your spending and end up overspending.

-        Every month, you need to calculate how much you will need to put towards your credit card payment to get out of debt quickly.

This was how you could use bank transfers to get the ultimate advantage. The next step is how you can become an authorized user.

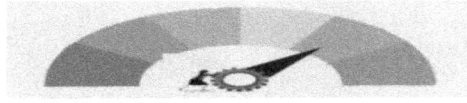

Chapter 6: Become An Authorized User

Becoming an authorized user is also a great technique that can be used to increase your credit score. It is because when you become an authorized user on a credit card, there is no credit check or the process which can make a card issuer deny you. It is not the legal responsibility of authorized users to pay for the charges they make while using the credit card.

The only person that is responsible is the original account holder. Even if you have the most terrible credit, someone can make you an authorized user. If the account holder keeps their credit well, this could also benefit you. This will increase your score as a result.

What is an authorized user?

An authorized user is a person who can make purchases on somebody else's credit account. For example, parents often add their teenage children as authorized users. This benefits them in building up their credit history. People also tend to add their partners and spouses as well.

An authorized user tends to get the credit cards connected to a credit line, but it is not their responsibility to pay off the charges they make on that card. The person whose name is on the card is responsible for paying off all the charges that an authorized user will make using their card.

If you ever decide to make a person your authorized user, you need to be very careful in choosing them because you will be responsible for paying off their debts. If you want to become an authorized user, it will be very beneficial for you, and in that case, you need to choose wisely whose account you want to get linked to as an authorized user. It would help if you chose those with a good credit score as it will also give a positive impression in your credit report.

The effect of an authorized user on your credit score:

There is proof of all the credit accounts that you were an authorized user in your credit history. The deal is that some issuers will report the account's information to the authorized users' credit reports. You would have to call the issuer to determine whether the authorized users' information is for your card.

Positive effect:

After the card issuer has reported the information to authorized users, it will affect each additional cardholder. There will be a positive effect if the primary cardholder takes care of the following things:

- Make their monthly payment on time.

- They have an appealing credit utilization rate.

The topics mentioned above will add up to the authorized user's credit limit, and they will have a positive payment history. This will also make their score excellent.

Negative effect:

Now it can have a negative impact as well if these things are there in the primary account holder's history:

- If they carry a high amount of debt, it can also hurt the authorized user.

- The high utilization ratio is also a factor that could negatively impact the authorized user.

- If they tend to miss many payments, it will have a negative effect.

The negative effect it leaves is in the form of a poor credit score for the authorized user.

The effect on the primary cardholder:

An authorized user's addition doesn't affect a primary cardholder's credit history or credit score if they do not make charges that the primary cardholder won't pay off. Only that can harm the primary cardholder's credit score or credit history.

How to become an authorized user?

Becoming an authorized user is a straightforward process, and almost every bank allows you to do that, and that too, with no extra charges except in some cases. After the simple process, you will receive a new credit card in the mail, and just like any new card, you will verify that it has been received to start using it.

Things to consider when becoming an authorized user:

It will help if you consider the following items into consideration when you are deciding to become an authorized user yourself:

-        Your first preference should be someone who has an excellent credit history. This is your number one priority, as primary cardholder credit and score

can impact your score, and you cannot impact their credit history or credit score.

- You also need to see if the primary account holder can manage their account with great responsibility or not.

- Now, this means that they should be the ones who pay their bills on time, have little debt, and their credit utilization ratio is less. It will be even better if it is near 20 percent.

- The next thing you need to consider is that the primary cardholder needs to have a relationship with you. It could be a close friend of yours or your family member.

- Lastly, you cannot pay anyone to make you their authorized user. FICO has strictly prohibited this act as it is done only by incrementing your score.

- This act is also known as piggy banking, and FICO will catch you off guard as they will see your relationship with the primary cardholder.

- Lastly, the primary cardholder should willingly make you an authorized user and not forcefully.

Becoming an authorized user could have both negative and positive effects. When trying to become one, you need to keep the abovementioned things. It's now time for the next step: to get secured credit cards.

Chapter 7: Get Secure Credit Cards:

Getting a secured credit card is another way to build your credit. In this, the payments are included in your credit report, and if you pay on time and have good management regarding the balances, this will increase your credit score. When a secured card is used responsibly, improving your financial history and credit score could be a great thing. This is a great way to boost up and rebuild your previous financial history and credit score, as it will give you the desired results in only 6 months.

What is a secure card?

A secured card is a type of card backed up by a cash deposit from the cardholder. Now the job of this secure credit card is to act as collateral on the account while providing security to prevent a situation where the cardholder cannot make payments. This type of credit card is the best for the individual who has suffered from limited credit history. It functions like any other credit card. This will establish your financial history as well. Secured credit cards typically have

lower credit limits and more fees than unsecured credit cards.

How it works:

Most credit cards that you see or use on your day-to-day basis are mostly unsecured types of credit cards. There is no credibility or assurance that you will pay the credit back to the company in an unsecured card. It is almost like a contract that you have made that you are not putting any of your assets to keep the agreement even though you need to pay every month, either full or partial. This is also why the interest rates are so high because these are related to unsecured debts, which are always high.

In simpler words, a secured credit card functions as a regular credit card that needs to be secured by a deposit. Now that deposit works as collateral if you do not pay your payments on time. The deposit falls somewhere between $200 and $500. Your credit limit is also the same amount as your deposit. You can use this just like any regular card you will use, but this doesn't mean that you end up paying your bills only by deposit every time. When you make purchases on the card, you need separate funds to pay your bills.

Other than this concept, you may use it like a regular credit card.

The impact of it on your credit score:

Building up your credit with a secured card is like building it up with a regular credit card. There are a few exceptions, but other than that, the impact of it on credit will have the same effects as a regular credit would do. No, the key here is to spend money in the most responsible way in which you can. You don't want to exceed your limit in any way. Your main motive should be only to purchase things you can pay for with cash.

The good thing is that you use your secured card almost every month to make small necessary purchases, and then after that, you tend to pay off your full balance. This gives the impression that you know how to manage your credit in the right way. As you know, your payment history is the most important factor for a good score; in this way, you will boost your credit score by paying the full payment on time and keeping your credit utilization low.

Things to look at when purchasing a secured credit card:

It would help if you saw certain things for yourself to choose the best secure credit card. Here are some tips to consider when getting a secure card.

\-   You need to look at the fees as some credit cards tend to charge an annual or a setup fee. You would not be charged if you chose not to take out advance cash or request balance transfers.

\-   You need to ensure your report is being delivered to all three major bureaus.

         Consider your credit card sources, as it needs to have a good reputation.

\-   You may find out about certain secured credit cards offering exceptional features, so do your research carefully.

\-   Credit unions offer lower interest rates than traditional banks, so it is better to check in with them.

How to use it effectively:

Now that you know how to choose your secure card, it is also vital for you to understand how to use it most

effectively to increase your credit. Here are some tips to help you use your secured credit card effectively.

-       You need to set up a budget to make only one or two small monthly purchases. This will also prevent you from overspending.

-       The best way to pay your balance is before the due date. This way, you won't have to pay the high-interest prices usually linked to secured cards.

-       Once you see progress in your credit score, you can return to an unsecured one.

Chapter 8: Use Free Apps to Help You Manage Your Boost Your Score

In this world, the use of digital devices has become a necessity. Your mobile phone can be highly beneficial for you when it comes to keeping an acceptable score because certain credit monitoring apps are free. They offer low-cost tools to manage, maintain, and improve your credit score. This is a fact that no matter how bad your credit score is, you can always improve it. You must know what your score is and what steps you can take to improve it.

Here is a list of specific apps to keep your credit manageable, improved, and intact.

Mint Money Manager:

This is a free app that is great for managing your debts. You can download it, which will keep you updated about your finances. It monitors your credit score and gives brief information about how you can improve your credit score. This brief information is very easy to understand, as well. Equifax is the credit model that is used to determine your score.

Another smart thing that this app does is that it also connects your investment accounts, bank accounts, and your credit cards. All the financial data is then combined in your Mint app. This app is great for checking all the situations of your finances in one place.

Debt tracker pro:

This is a reliable app if you want to check your various debts. You can include many things, including your credit card, lines of credit, or even some mortgages. As it tells you about the internet rates of cost of credit and inters rates, it becomes convenient for you to decide which debts to pay first. As you know that your credit utilization also matters a lot in your credit scores, this app ensures you keep the utilization at its minimum. It helps you in the monitoring of credit utilization.

Credit Karma:

This app is very user friendly, and it helps you in monitoring your score well. It will give you a weekly report of your credit report and as well as your credit score. They also have a service that can break down all the factors contributing to your credit score.

In this, you will know the type of spending you are doing better and how it impacts your credit score. All these things are enlisted in the form of a credit Karma report.

This app tracks your credit scores from Equifax and TransUnion. The two main crediting bureaus make up your scores and reports. You can also review your credit reports that have errors and are based on some misinformation. Another great thing about this app is that it lets you file a dispute directly through the app. This technique is very convenient as it saves you a lot of time and prevents the hassle.

Credit.com:

This is an app that makes use of the Experian score. This app is free, and you can use this with great ease. You will receive a grade after signing up for this. This app makes up your credit score by analyzing the following things:

- Payment history

- Account mix

- Debt usage

- Credit age

It also gives you a grade along with the score. This app is very convenient due to the visual aids that make it easier to learn certain factors, such as how they calculated your score and whether you improved it. You will also be able to see your credit mistakes, and you can find a way to fix them. You can access your entire credit profile, including an insight that will tell you what condition it's in compared to your peers. It will give you accurate information on your current credit score and how to improve it.

Experian:

Experian is one of three main crediting bureaus that make up your score. They also have a free app that you can use. Their credit rating model is what is used by so many monitoring apps. The Experian app will monitor all the possible changes in your credit profile, and it will give you advice on how your financial health changes.

You will have a push option to see your score whenever changes are made to your score. This makes it easier to note the changes and improvements in your credit score. This app updates your overall credit almost every month. It will automatically be updated after 30 days.

This app also comes with Experian Boost, which can boost your score. It alerts you exactly when changes in your score occur, and it will then offer you some suggested credit cards based on your overall score.

TransUnion:

This is also the third main crediting bureau, and it has an app that you can easily download on your phone. It will allow you to see your credit score according to the Transunion credit reports. You can see your credit score as well as your credit reports daily. It also has a debt analysis tool, which lets you see your debt-to-income ratio. You will also be able to see public records associated with your name.

Apps are another great way to keep your credit scores high. The good thing about them is that they are mostly free, and all you must do is download them. You can choose whichever app you like, and your score tracking game will be done much easier.

Now it is time for the next step in increasing your score, and it is to have hard inquiries removed, which you didn't allow for pulling your credit.

Chapter 9: Have Hard Inquiries Removed You Didn't Allow for Pulling Your Credit

A credit inquiry is a record of when someone requests your credit file. If there is any hard inquiry, then it can affect your credit score. You don't have to worry about single hard inquiries as it won't impact your eligibility for a new credit card.

If the hard inquiry in your credit report is the one you did authorize or apply for, an account is considered legitimate, and it could take almost two years to get fully removed from your credit report.

There is also a chance that there might also be some unauthorized inquiries. This is why you always need to check your reports thoroughly. The best way to do this is to review your credit reports regularly to avoid such inconveniences. In case you find one, then there is a solution for that. You should file a dispute with the credit bureau that generated that in the first place. It would help if you asked the bureau to remove the inquiry. It would be best to remove these inaccurate inquiries as they impact your score.

The impact on your credit score:

When an inquiry is reported, you will see an immediate decrease in your score. Although it will be a minor decrease, it can last a year. You can make this a minimum impact on your score by keeping your inquiries within a 30-day frame. This way, even if you have multiple inquiries, it will count only as one hard inquiry. Your score may decrease to 1-5 points, but you can continually improve it by paying on time and doing other things to ensure you do.

Here is how you can dispute inaccurate inquiries.

Review your credit reports:

It would help if you created a habit of reviewing your credit reports from the three major credit bureaus: Equifax, TransUnion, and Experian. These credit bureaus would not know the incorrect information unless you flag it.

Now to check the incorrect hard inquiries, you need to focus on this section:

-       Credit inquiries

-       Hard inquiries

-       Requests which are viewed by others

\-   Regular inquiries

There would also be a section for soft inquiries. You don't have to focus on what's written there as it won't affect your score, but it is better to review it only. You can regularly view your credit reports through the apps mentioned in the previous chapters.

Look for the unauthorized or incorrect hard inquiry:

You can get the hard inquiry removed from your credit report under two conditions. The two conditions are:

\-   If you didn't apply for a new credit account, then you can get it removed

\-   If you didn't authorize the credit inquiry, then you can get it removed

You could not remove the hard inquiries if you did any of the actions mentioned above. It will remain on your reports, and it will be a part of your credit history. It will fall from your credit history after at least two years.

There can be some inquiries that may sound a bit suspicious. This means that you might not recognize

the company's exact name of who inquired, or you encountered more inquiries than you expected, do not think of it as a scam or a fraud.

If an unauthorized hard inquiry is on your credit reports, it could happen due to various reasons:

-       A credit account was applied for by using your information, which someone did fraudulently. When this happens, then this could be a sign that someone stole your identity. You don't want any further misuse of information, and for that reason, you need to consider the following things:

•   You need to put a fraud alert on your credit reports.

•   The Federal Trade Commission usually deals with theft, and you need to report your case to them.

•   You can even file a police report for this reason.

•   You can also contact the creditor if a fraudulent account appears on your reports. If this happens, then ask the creditor to close your account.

-       A creditor pulled your credit even though you didn't give your consent to do so. If this happens, you

need to dispute it, as it will negatively impact your scores.

-        The credit bureau mistakenly added the inquiry to your credit report. You need to do the same thing here and try to improve your credit, and you don't want to damage it further.

Fill it with the corresponding bureau:

The credit bureaus must investigate if you find an error in your credit reports and any unauthorized hard inquiries. It is also their job to correct incorrect information.

As you know that there are three major credit bureaus, which include:

-        Experian

-        TransUnion

-        Equifax

You can file a dispute with any of the three creditors. They must have an inaccurate hard inquiry recorded for you on its corresponding credit report to dispute. As mentioned before, Credit Karma the app will let you dispute through the app. You can even fight

online in many ways, but it is also advised to mail your dispute to the respective agencies with inaccurate inquiries. After the investigation, if the credit bureaus find out that the inquiry wasn't authorized, it will be removed from your credit report immediately.

This was how you could tackle a challenging setback on your credit report, such as a hard inquiry. Tax liens are often also mentioned in your credit report, even though they have been paid. The next step will tell you how you can remove it.

Chapter 10: Have Tax Liens That Are Paid Removed

Tax liens are said to be the most difficult debt that could be on your credit reports. The reason for this is that it involves the government. The government takes priority over all the creditors. You will have difficulty dealing with the government as they expect you to pay fully. Paying the total amount owed is also a way to remove the tax liens. Tax liens are for public record. Government agencies place tax liens when people fail to pay local and state taxes. People often think they got a tax lien because they did not pay the government's income tax. This is not the case, as the government can also give you a tax lien if you do not pay their property tax.

How to remove:
Here is how you can remove the tax liens:

Appeal the lien:
The IRS will only remove the tax lien if you prove you are correct. Here are the specific conditions which will tell you whether you can get the tax liens removed or not:

- The tax debt is paid in full.

- The lien was falsely filed.

- The IRS did not follow accurate processes.

- The 10-year statute of limitations on collecting tax debt has expired.

After you have received the lien notice, you can file for a collection due process, which the appeals office will hear. You need to do this process in at least 30 days.

The withdrawal of the linen:

The withdrawal of the linen is great for the stressed-out taxpayers out there. When a tax lien is withdrawn, then there is no proof of it if even it was there or not. This can only happen if the person paying the tax pays off the lien. If it was wrongly filled, then it could be withdrawn as well. The withdrawal could be made if your debt is $ 25000 or less. This is also known as the Fresh Start Initiative. You can also negotiate, and a compromise could be made with the IRS in which the taxpayer pays a lesser amount, but it is considered full payment.

Releasing the lien:

Releasing the lien is linked to the first idea. If you fall in the category of a new initiative and your balance is less than the required amount, which is $25000, you can get the lien quickly released. If you do not request it on your own, it will release instinctively after 30 days once you have paid the full payment. When a lien gets released, it detaches from your property, car, and other assets. Once it's removed, then you must send its copy to the bureaus so that they can update your credit report.

Lien subordination:

Lien subordination is another way to take care of the tax lien. Another creditor's job is to subordinate the IRS's interest in the property to move ahead. This process is very complex and doesn't always work, so I recommend you choose the option from the previously mentioned ways.

After the IRS has removed your tax lien, you will receive a notification of the release of the tax lien's withdrawal. You need to contact all three agencies to know that your reports are updated.

How to avoid:

The best way to avoid tax liens is, in fact, by paying your taxes on time. This statement is simple, but not many people stick to this entirely. Always file your taxes and do not give the government a chance to interfere. The damage they do to your credit is crucial even though they can be removed. If you find it difficult to pay taxes on time, you can surely take other steps to avoid government involvement that happens through a tax lien. There is always a solution to every problem, but that doesn't mean you stop caring about your concerns.

These are the ten steps that will bring a positive change in your credit score by increasing it.

You Must Have Patient

Achieving a good credit score is not an overnight step; it takes consistency, dedication, patience, and smart decisions. You need to start taking the appropriate ten steps to boost your score you just read in this book starting today.

These ten steps are simple but not easy. You need to ensure that you take prevention to avoid getting into situations that will negatively impact your credit score.

You can fix bad credit by rebuilding or improving it with average credit and financial history. It is important to take any action to do it as it will benefit every aspect of your life.